FACING YOURSELF

By: Sharon Hatch

Dedication

I have honestly struggled with who to dedicate my book to. Number one is easy- for all that has been and all that there is to come is God.

Therefore, it feels appropriate to mention my inner child who helped me survive and got me to the place where I stand today. I recognize my adult self to have the courage to step out of all shadows and roles and share my truth. I guess, I am dedicating this book to me.

Lastly, I must also give thanks to the Twelve Step Programs for giving me a blueprint for Life.

LETTER FROM THE AUTHOR

I hope my story plants seeds of inspiration and hope in your spirit. As I write this letter, I'm in such awe of how amazing life is, how amazing God is. The odds were stacked against me after my brain aneurysm. Most do not survive; yet I did. I was definitely at a crossroads in life during that time, trying to understand my purpose for still being alive. Every time I reflected on the question, the one thing that came to me repeatedly was to write a book sharing my story and wisdom.

I believe with all my heart that this book is the very reason I am alive. It was validated to me even more the moment I started entertaining the curiosities around writing a book. I mentioned the idea to my niece who just so happened to know a Ghostwriter and Publisher, Shareen Rivera. The instant we spoke on the phone, I knew intuitively that it was her that I needed to use to help me write my book. She had similar life experiences as me and understood many of the principles I lived by. As we continued on this journey, experiences in my life started unfolding in her own life in the most uncanny way, the timing almost aligning with each section we were writing. Certain topics she didn't have an understanding of, she now did, and was able to better articulate what I felt at the soul level.

As if that wasn't enough validation, through this process, I've been able to see myself in a different light that I haven't experienced. This has allowed me to be open to receiving peace in relationships that were once strained. I've been able to step outside of the shadows I lived in all my life and learn what it means to believe in yourself and support yourself regardless of who else is supporting you. It's been such a healing process for me and the beauty of it is that I never expected to get this much healing from it. This is why I know that what you are holding in your hands right now is the point for me still being here. I pray that whoever picks this book up receives the healing from it as I did and that my words in these pages continue to do so long after I'm gone.

TWELVE AL ANON STEPS

1. We admitted we were powerless over alcohol—that our lives had become unmanageable.

2. Came to believe that a Power greater than ourselves could restore us to sanity.

3. Made a decision to turn our will and our lives over to the care of God as we understood Him.

4. Made a searching and fearless moral inventory of ourselves.

5. Admitted to God, to ourselves, and to another human being the exact nature of our wrongs.

6. Were entirely ready to have God remove all these defects of character.

7. Humbly asked Him to remove our shortcomings.

8. Made a list of all persons we had harmed and became willing to make amends to them all.

9. Made direct amends to such people wherever possible, except when to do so would injure them or others.

10. Continued to take personal inventory and when we were wrong promptly admitted it.

11. Sought through prayer and meditation to improve our conscious contact with God as we understood Him, praying only for knowledge of His will for us and the power to carry that out.

12. Having had a spiritual awakening as the result of these steps, we tried to carry this message to others, and to practice these principles in all our affairs.

A journey of a
thousand miles starts
with the first step.

- *Lao Tzu*

Introduction

Every single person alive wants to be happy at some fundamental level, whatever that may look like, and we all crave inner peace. If our thoughts are what determines how we feel, then how do we unravel the wiring of our mind? How do we undo all the negative thinking, forget and unsee all the trauma and sadness? Ultimately, the real question that many wonder is how do we become happy and free again after experiencing so much pain? Perhaps life is a journey of figuring those questions out for ourselves; awakening enough to finding clues along our way that guide each of us to a tool that can help. What if the pain serves a purpose? What if life isn't about escaping the pain but learning from it? Maybe the lessons are some of the tools we seek.

For me to have any chance of maintaining my vibration and having what I call a good day, I must stick with my morning routine. When I wake up, I head to what I call my Zen room, with my coffee, my Bible, and my daily readings to meet with my Higher Power, who I call God. I then go through the first three out of the twelve steps for Al-Anon. They are one of the tools that work for me and have become my guide for life on how to deal with any and everything.

I know now that nothing in this life is by pure chance or coincidence. Everything has a deeper spiritual meaning-divine synchronicities if you will. I've learned that if you're patient and open enough, you will see what the meanings are. Mike, my late husband, was the clue that led me to the twelve Al-Anon steps. Little did I know at the time that Al-Anon would be the place that gave me the blueprint on how to live my life, how to heal through forgiveness and free myself, and how to love myself enough so that I can experience true love. In some way or another, I've experienced every kind of pain or loss imaginable as if I've lived hundreds of lives in this one lifetime, but I've been fortunate enough to liberate myself from the bondage that came with it. Everything that happens can be reduced to surrendering to God, having faith, and being love. It may sound simple, too simple some would say, but believe me when I say applying those three steps take intention and work every day.

The unraveling of our inner world happens when we face ourselves- the good, the bad, and the ugly. It is through this process that we have the power to recreate everything in our lives. Nothing is set in stone. Nothing is permanent. Everything is ever changing to the winds of energy that command the movement, and you are the one that has the ability to determine what that energy that is. My intention for this book is to repurpose my life's experiences for others as a token of gratitude to the Universe, and a clue for those reading, just as Mike was to me, that there is light at the end of whatever tunnel you may find yourself in.

"When my former husband was dying, I asked him how I'd know he was around. He thought about it and told me that whenever I see a red cardinal to know that it was him. Now, anytime I'm at a crossroads or need answers or validation I see a red cardinal or a feather of one. I know it's him and a sign to lead me down my destined path, and as I continue on that particular path, I always later find out the reason why. Each time, I'm in awe of the beauty of how it all unfolds."

- **Sharon Hatch**

Dear God,
I am powerless and my life is unmanageable without your help
and guidance.
I come to you today because I believe
that You can restore and renew me to meet my needs today.

Since I cannot manage my life or affairs,
I have decided to give them to You.
I put my life, my will, my thoughts,
my desires and ambitions in Your hands.
I give You all of me: the good and the bad,
the character defects and shortcomings,
my selfishness, resentments and problems.
I know that You will work them out in accordance with Your plan.

Such as I am, take and use me in Your service.
Guide and direct my ways and show me what to do for You.

I cannot control or change my friends or loved ones,
so I release them into Your care for Your loving arms to do with
as You will.

Just keep me loving and free from judging them.
If they need changing, God You'll have to do it; I can't.
Just make me willing and ready to be of service to You, to have my
shortcomings removed, and to do my best.

Help me to see how I have harmed others and make me willing to make amends to them all.

Keep me ever mindful of thoughts and actions that harm myself or others, and which separate me from Your light, love and spirit. And when I commit these errors, make me aware of them and help me to admit each one promptly.

*I am seeking to know You better,
to love You more.*

*I am seeking the knowledge of Your will for me
and the power to carry it out.*

Fear of not being loved, of
abandonment, of being thought
to be selfish- is the main thing
that keeps us vulnerable and
bound in the chains of
emotional dependence.
Therefore, our two most
difficult challenges are to truly
believe it's okay for us to be
ourselves and to learn to live
with, move through, and heal
our fears.

-Sue Thoele

To forgive is to set
a prisoner free and
discover that the
prisoner was you.

- Lewis B. Smedes

Abandonment

As a little girl, I'd sit for hours looking out the window waiting and watching for someone to come home. As a grown woman, and then again as a mother, I found myself, reliving the same experience- looking out the window, waiting and watching for my husband and then children to come home. The thing is, when you're in it, living out the residual effects of your childhood trauma, you don't know it and you can't even see it. You're completely blinded by your pain and fragmented beliefs that were created from fear. Fear of what? Maybe it's fear of being left and abandoned; fear of being alone; fear of rejection; fear of not being wanted.

I had no clue that I chose to marry a man that would not only fill the void of my parents but also leave me feeling the same way- abandoned. When you have missing pieces inside of you, you tend to attract people that do as well, except their missing pieces fits perfectly with yours. For me at the time, he was my missing piece. When we married, he was starting to build his career as an executive of a company which required him to travel which meant he was gone for large portions of time. This was time I was forced to spend alone caring for our children, waiting on pins and needles for my husband to come home, just as I did as a child waiting for my parents. Although, at first, he was gone due to work, the end result was always me being alone, and it triggered my inner child that still remembered the days of being alone.

When my mom was pregnant with me, she was diagnosed with some form of female cancer. In those days, that felt like a death sentence. With no tools or guidance, her coping mechanism was to drown herself in alcohol which in-turn resulted in her not being home much. My older sister, at only six years old, only four years older than I was, was left caring for me. My father was also gone, working and what not, but the permanent feeling of being left was engrained in my soul from the time I was a child. It left a void and a flawed "picker" if you will of choosing the same type of people to fill that void. A void that would continue to be triggered until I paid enough attention to heal it.

So, what do you do when your husband is always gone? Well, you try to be better. I tried to be prettier, be more fun, be sexier, keep the house cleaner, cook better, be more submissive- you think it, I tried it.

When nothing else worked, then I started hating myself and that feeling of not being good enough was magnified. I allowed my self-worth to be determined by him and his life. So, I did this little dance- a dance that continued until I stopped to confront it. But it is a process to stop the dance, and it takes us sometimes going through cycles of pain until we realize that we have the power to stop.

So, what do you do when you feel bad about yourself? Well, you join a church and turn to God. I became obsessed with church and religion and was hardcore about it all. "Perhaps if I became holier, the most Christian-like woman, try harder, pray the right prayer, help enough people, be perfect like Jesus, then, maybe then, God would save my marriage and my husband will want to be with me," was what I told myself. If he doesn't, then it's God's will, but my duty was to eat, think, sleep God's word, and I did. I did so much that I was so busy being involved in the church that I wasn't present to see how it was affecting my children. I didn't see how it was a distraction from me dealing with my own internal issues of not being happy in my marriage. I didn't see that I still wasn't facing myself.

Instead, I was going through the motions of what looked right in the eyes of the church. Whatever my husband said or did, went without any disagreement or argument from me, in hopes of getting him back. The insanity of it all was that my husband had already moved out, but since the church I attended told me that God hates divorce, I stayed at home with the kids praying for his return. Meanwhile, he was off living another life, with another woman somewhere else.

Him meeting me at church on Sundays was the lifeline, enough of a bread crumb that gave me hope to hang on. There I was, every Sunday, in the front of the church as one of the prayer warriors, praying for people, and he was in the band, while my life was in shambles. I was using religion as a way of not dealing with my issues, and I know many people do that as well. The thing is all of us were born into this world perfect and whole as we are, in the image of God, which is perfection. Then life happens and somewhere along the way we forget who we are, and sometimes it requires us to go beyond our comfort zone to heal the issues that cloud our sight from seeing and remembering who we are. If you want them to be gone, if you want to feel different, then you must face them. I remember a story of a praying man that expresses this perfectly.

"A man was trapped in his house during a flood. He began praying to God to rescue him. He had a vision in his head of God's hand reaching down from heaven and lifting him to safety. The water started to rise in his house. His neighbor urged him to leave and offered him a ride to safety. The man yelled back, "I am waiting for God to save me." The neighbor then drove off in his pick-up truck.

The man continued to pray and hold on to his vision. As the water began rising in his house, he had to climb up to the roof. A boat came by with some people heading for safe ground. They yelled at the man to grab a rope they were ready to throw and take him to safety. He told them that he was waiting for God to save him. They shook their heads and moved on.

The man continued to pray, believing with all his heart that he would be saved by God. The floodwaters continued to rise. A helicopter flew by, and a voice came over a loudspeaker offering to lower a ladder and take him off the roof. The man waved the helicopter away, shouting back that he was waiting for God to save him. The helicopter left. The flooding water came over the roof and caught him up and swept him away. He drowned.

When he reached heaven and asked, "God, why did you not save me? I believed in you with all my heart. Why did you let me drown?" God replied, "I sent you a pick-up truck, a boat, and a helicopter and you refused all of them. What else could I possibly do for you?"

I think of this when I think of dealing with childhood trauma, because so many of us, including my past self, think that if we just pray harder, God will miraculously heal us. It doesn't work that way. You must do the work and reach for the tools that God will bring your way once you ask and are ready to receive them. The tools for me came when Mike led me to Al-Anon, not through his words but through his example and undeniable light. When Mike and I were friends, I would bring him into my prayer meetings. While everyone else was casting out demons, throwing holy oils and water in the air, and speaking out loud in tongues, Mike quietly sat on the sidelines praying the Serenity and Lord's prayer. I'm sure it looked crazy to anyone on the outside, and it partially was. I used to think that I could help him grow, which is funny to me now because during that time I couldn't even tell you what my favorite color was. I hadn't met myself at the most basic level. It's so ironic how the tables turn on you in life when you don't know what you don't know. It turned out that it was him who would help me grow and heal in so many ways. Mike's light led me to be curious and wanting to learn what his secret to peace and happiness was. He brought me to my first AA meeting which led me to Al-Anon. It was there that I learned the twelve steps. It was there that I met people that could guide me and show me the way. It was there that I found myself finally ready to receive the support to face myself.

When I finally was ready to follow through with a divorce, the pastor from the church made one last attempt to "save" me by making a special trip to my house and lay the guilt on thick about proceeding with a divorce. Despite the situation falling under the category of a rightful divorce according to the laws of the church, it was still frowned upon. I knew that the pastor meant well, but I also knew that he didn't know better and that he was at a different place than me in his journey. I finally knew my truth and felt comfortable for the first time with my decision regardless of who was against me, and it was empowering to say the least. Once I faced myself and started this journey of self-discovery and awareness and healing, I was soon faced with the next layer of abandonment. That was, I had now become the one abandoning. I had abandoned the church and felt like that meant I was abandoning Jesus which, according to many church going Christians, comes with its own set of consequences.

With each trauma comes another layer to face within ourselves. The layer of abandonment was so deep in me and connected to the next layer of people-pleasing. From there it goes on and on and on, but the root always remained at abandonment. When mentoring people, I often use these cute wooden stacking dolls that I have as an example of healing from abandonment and codependency. As you open the largest doll, which symbolizes the doll that we hide underneath, the face we show the world, there's another doll to open right after, and it continues until you find the smallest doll that no longer opens. That smallest doll for me represents the inner child that lies within my core that holds all the sadness and pain and trauma- that still remembers. For me, it was the little girl that hid in the dark closet waiting for her parents to come home. It is that inner child that is connected to the root issue beneath each layer and getting back to that part of ourselves helps us face ourselves with the compassion and love that we deserve and yearn for. Opening each doll to get to the next inside symbolizes the courage it requires to have my inner child step out of her comfortable corner in the dark closet and into the light of the world.

Experiencing self-loathing in the form of guilt caused me to realize that it was time for me to go through the first three Al-Anon steps and do a self-inventory in terms of my relationship with God. I needed to get back to my truth. What does God mean to me? Who is God? How can I surrender to God and display the faith I needed in my life to release the burden of living my life for others? How can I love, be love, and love myself? I think that many people grow up having an idea of God, but feel that they are too miniscule, not important enough, to matter in comparison to all the issues God must deal with in the entire Universe. People have this distant connection with God, almost as if they're staring at a beautiful picture of a faraway exotic island that they think they'll never travel to, because the idea of it is simply overwhelmed by all the HOW's. How can

I afford a trip like that? How can I take time away to even go? How can I feel like I even belong at a place like that, because people that travel to those exotic places are wealthy and successful? How can I escape the judgement of my friends and family if I go? Like everything else in life, once you shift the perspective of what you're focusing on, your belief can change. Start looking at the how's as representing Honest, Open, and Willing, and fill in the rest of the sentence to give you that necessary shift.

Sometimes when you are the picture inside the frame, you can't see what others see. You need someone on the outside, that you trust, to tell you what they see. That is why Al-Anon was so crucial in my life, because for the first time I had people that I trusted to tell me what they saw. I have many people that reach out to me for help, who think that I can solve their problems, or that there's a magic thing to do or a book to read that can solve their problems. The truth is, there is nothing or no one that can solve your problems, but you and God. You have to be willing to do the work. You have to be willing to invest in your healing with your energy, time, and effort. I tell these people frequently that if they are serious about wanting to change, then meet me at an Al-Anon meeting and we'll go from there. Most of them never do. Perhaps they haven't experienced enough pain or maybe they're not ready to do the work. I don't know what it is, but I do know that most don't take the first step towards change.

Change in any aspect of our life requires us to take a step outside the edge of our comfort zone. It requires us to get used to being uncomfortable, to being vulnerable in ways that we never experienced, to face ourselves in that place. Al-Anon's first step is to admit we are powerless, and it is in that place of vulnerability with our ego put aside, in surrendering, that we can clearly see ourselves. Often, what we see is not pretty, and that's ok. Because it is only there that we can truly see what needs to be done to heal, to change, to recreate ourselves from a place of love instead of living a life of trying to fit into a mold that was given to us from trauma. Isn't this what life is all about- the hope for more- the possibility that something else, another way of being, of living is possible? I'm here to tell you, it is.

QUESTIONS TO FACE YOURSELF

What are you powerless over?

What are you trying to control?

How is your life unmanageable?

Grace means that
all your mistakes
now serve a purpose
instead of serving
shame.

- Brene Brown

Moms Are
People Too

If there is ever a time that a woman needs her mother, is it not when she too becomes a mother? In many of us women, within this need, lie layers of emotions that are slowly peeled away as we experience our lives as mothers, wives, and our role in this world. With time and overcoming much heartbreak, loss, sadness, betrayals, sickness, and pain we find ourselves looking back and reflecting, yet this time, through different eyes; eyes that now understand. Within this understanding I found myself being able to have compassion for my mother and even more importantly, I found myself being able to forgive her.

"Forgiveness is the fragrance the violet sheds on the heel that has crushed it."

- Mark Twain

I was able to forgive her for not being around as a child because of the demons she was battling. I may not have understood her choices, but I can recognize and understand the struggle as a mother having to parent while fighting to heal my own internal demons. I was blessed with the opportunity to care for my mother before she passed away. For the first time in my adult life we were able to get to know one another with mutual understanding and respect that brought us a whole new sense of appreciation for one another.

Growing up, like most children that experience neglect, I didn't understand why things were the way they were. I blamed myself. I blamed myself for my parents not being around and spending time with me. I blamed myself when I later learned of my mom developing cervical cancer after giving birth to me even though it was never proven that the two things were related. I blamed myself for my parents not staying together. It's crazy the things we tell ourselves when we're children that we continue to hold onto as adults and become part of our belief system about ourselves.

To cause more confusion to the already existing chaos that was my life, my father decided to kidnap me and my sister and take us across country to California. My dad met a woman named, Shirley, that he met during a vacation he took us on in this old bread truck he converted into a camper. They hit it off and I suppose she gave him hope for more, to believe in love again, and he risked it all to have it again in his life. I was six years old and didn't understand anything that was happening, but it seemed like we were saying goodbye to family and friends at a party one evening. My mom was no where to be found, but that seemed to be the norm those days. The next day my dad loaded us in the converted bread truck, and we started the twenty-five-day journey from Massachusetts to California, where Shirley lived. I wanted my mom with us and felt pains of sadness as we got further and further away from the only place I knew as home. It wouldn't be until five years later that I would return to finally see my mom who, by that time, was so deep and distracted living her own life that we she barely saw my sister and I and we spent our entire trip with our grandmother.

The long-distance trip didn't go as smoothly as my dad had planned, and the converted camper broke down in Pennsylvania, but my dad got it up and running some how and hung a sign up in the back that read, "CALIFORNIA OR BUST," and he meant it. Hell or high water, he was determined to get us to California to start our new life. Despite missing my mom, I held the excitement of a six-year-old on an adventure, and both my sister and I had such a good time for the first time in our lives not only spending so much quality time with our dad but also visiting all the landmark places, national parks, and Indian Reservations. We gained the same hope as our father that maybe life would be better in California.

We found that to be short lived though as we found ourselves at a seedy motel in San Jose, California that had an unusable pool and rundown sign in front. The saving grace for us was that there were many other children that lived there with their families too. Our dad got a job at the San Jose Mercury newspaper and worked the night shift, and once again, we found ourselves alone caring for ourselves. My sister found a few babysitting jobs after school or during the evenings, and that left me alone in the motel room. My spirit yearned for someone to talk to, to tell me what was going on, to guide me. Even more so, my spirit craved to be heard, for someone to listen to me. In an attempt to fill this need as a child, I'd line up my dolls and talk to them. I'd give them advise and tell them what to do. I'd tell them all the things that I needed to hear. It wasn't until two years later that my dad married and moved us in with Shirley, and I finally was able to experience stability as well as a mother figure in my life. She taught me what it meant to be a productive member of society, to be a lady. She not only talked to me about life but listened to me. She filled the void of my mother, and I feel blessed for that. Perhaps her presence helped stop the cycle that my mother started.

I recognized that my mother was a mirror for me to see into both realms of the past and future, of what was and what could be if I allowed it. As I held her hand as she took her last breaths and left this physical world, I cried bittersweet tears; tears of sadness because our time together was cut short and tears of liberation, through forgiveness and a grateful heart that we made peace in our relationship. How easy it is to lose ourselves in the shadows of the world while trying to numb ourselves.

How hard it is to live up the superhuman expectation children have of their mother and men have of their wives. Often, no matter how hard we try, it is never good enough. Someone is always left disappointed, if not our children, then our husbands or family. For years, I've found myself running in circles chasing perfection, trying to get my fill of validation to satisfy my codependency addiction. So many mothers are doing the same thing, and the question that we must ask ourselves is when does it ever end? Better yet, how do we heal while living in a role that requires you to be superhuman?

"There is no greater blessing a mother can give her daughter than a reliable sense of the veracity of her own intuition."

- Clarissa Pinkola Estes

Unfortunately, there is no magic handbook that falls into our lap with all the answers, but I have learned the power in taking a step back to think before reacting or making important decisions. I learned the hardwiring in my brain programmed from my childhood defaults to people pleasing. It defaults to fill my hunger pains for validation, at whatever cost. I also understand that to overcome and reprogram my mind to feel differently I first had to learn to be comfortable in my own skin, with my own decisions, because from there everyone else will follow. It is in this place that, once again, the Al-Anon steps walked me through the journey of healing and self-love.

All my life it was so easy to give grace to people that treated me incorrectly or did me wrong. Grace to both my parents for leaving me and my sister alone for a large part of my childhood. Grace for putting me on standby as a child. I desperately craved a normal family structure. I didn't like the disorganization and not knowing of where mom or dad was. I had to teach myself the best I could when it came to life skills. No one was watching us. A feeling validated when my mother attempted to show a picture of me as a child and after a closer look, it turned out to be my cousin. My short pixie cut haircut made it difficult to mistake me for anyone else, but what I realized was there were hardly any pictures of me as a child because like I said, I was on standby; yet I managed to give grace.

Grace to my ex-husband for being absent for most of our marriage. Grace to my children anytime they gave me a hard time. Yet, I couldn't find it in me to extend the same type of grace to myself. I exhausted my energy running in circles striving for perfection out of attempts from my codependency to keep my first husband home. How many of us women do this?

As nurturers we give grace, and extend compassion and love to others, but when it comes to ourselves, it seems impossible to do the same thing. Would you speak to your best friend the way you speak to yourself? Would you advise your best friend to be as hard on themselves as you are on yourself? As the first four steps in Al-Anon advises, accepting ourselves as we are, surrendering to God in full faith, is the path towards love, self-love. In this state you can begin to

create from a place of trueness and authenticity, free from the tainted remnants of our trauma. Just because you can do something doesn't necessarily mean you should do something. Remember, us mothers are people too.

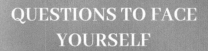

QUESTIONS TO FACE
YOURSELF

What do you do because you don't feel ok?

What are your survival mechanisms?

Why can't you pause?

Who then is in charge of your life?

We are the ones, the only ones, who can now pick up the pieces for ourselves and heal the wounded child. Other people can be there as guides, as friends, as therapists, but the work has to be done by us. We are the ones who have to get up every morning and deal with our pain and we are the ones who have to turn to our inner child in pain, holding and loving that child the way she or he should have been held and loved years ago.

- Mary Jane Williams

Self-Love

Life is nothing more than a reflection of ourselves. The way we love others; what we see in others; the people, places, and things we attract- everything is reflecting some part of ourselves back to us. I know for myself, it's taken a large portion of my life to understand this but I am grateful for this lesson because I know so many live their whole life never understanding this universal rule. Once you do though, life becomes a classroom, even a game if you will, all leading you to an important destination- to A Higher Power (who I call God) and to love yourself more.

As an adult, I thought that I survived my childhood and that it was done and over with; yet I was so far from done. The residual energy from all the trauma was still very much real, and it wanted to be recognized so that I could heal it. How do you heal it if you don't know it's there though? Often, we become so blinded to what life is that we can't even see what's possible. I had become so desensitized to being abandoned that when I got married to my first husband, and he was gone all the time doing his own thing, I immediately went into my "fix-it" bag and searched for ways to be better. This was my go-to behavior that I learned as a child. If only I was a better child, made better grades, was prettier, helped out more, the list goes on, just maybe my parents would stay around.

When my marriage ended failing anyway, I was drowning in denial and illusions of what I wanted it to be. Even though he was never home and was living with his new girlfriend, I held onto the hope of "maybe one day". I turned to religion to fix my problems, and it was just me, my kids, and the church. Healing yourself as a single mom is no joke at all. Having little eyes on you while trying to navigate through your mental muddle is hard. The thing is, you can't truly experience self-love until you face the pain that is holding you down and heal yourself. Once you heal yourself, you start to know yourself, and when that happens anything is possible.

I was elated to be a mother. My first son, Vince, was such a beautiful baby, and my ex-husband and I were so happy and full of love for this child. I finally had a family of my own. One thing was for sure: I was going to be there for this child, and I was going to do everything in my power to make this family work. Of course, life had other plans for me. I hadn't quite realized yet that I had married a workaholic.

My first husband was determined to climb the corporate ladder and be as successful as he could be at any cost, and that meant a lot of time traveling for work away from the family. Because he was adopted, he always had a chip on his shoulder. Whether it was to prove to himself, his adoptive family, or his real family, wherever they were, that he was worth something. Probably a little of all of it. I just wished he realized he was always worth something, with or without the job. Just as I needed to know I was worth something – I think we all do – somewhere sick people chose sick people to replay it all – even determined to not. I wish he didn't have so much to prove. I think within the first week or two of Vincent being born, he was gone on business for three weeks to Japan. I was alone once again, this time with a newborn child. I had to have my ten-year-old nephew hang out with me so that I wouldn't be totally alone. What is it in the face of being alone that we run from? Why are we so scared of ourselves? I look back with so much compassion at this younger version of myself and my heart goes out to her, because I remember how painful it was being alone and not feeling like I was enough- not even for me. It was around this time that I started to suspect that my husband was having affairs outside of our marriage. I didn't ever know for sure at the time, but the markers were there. Late nights out drinking with "friends," estranged love at home, never seeing him much. My notion of the perfect family was slipping away by the day, but I was addicted to him. Maybe if I was just the perfect wife he would come home more, or drink less, or work less. I told myself these lies for years, but I didn't know what else to do. I didn't have the tools yet to operate in a healthy way toward myself, no-less my own family. As with any long journey into unknown terrain, you need tools, and the self-love journey is no different. The tools in this journey though are gained through our experiences of heartbreak. It would be another decade before I even got a glimpse of what it meant to break the cycle of searching outside of myself for fulfillment.

"I say the universe speaks to us, always, first in whispers. If you don't pay attention to the whisper, then it's like getting a brick upside your head. You don't pay attention to that—the brick wall falls. So, I ask people, 'What are the whispers? What's whispering to you now?'"

- Oprah Winfrey

My search for outside validation did not stop with a sudden event, rather, it was more of a process through a sequence of multiple events over a good length of time. It came through forgiving others for hurting me because forgiveness is really for yourself. It frees your energy from holding on. It came through letting go and just being and relying on faith. It came through my daily disciplines. It came through a lifetime of learning through the shifts of life.

My relationship with myself took time that didn't start until I was able to start giving myself time. Imagine being in an intimate relationship with someone, but never giving them time with you. Every time you are alone with them, you run in the opposite direction. Every time you get an opportunity to talk with them and learn them, you shut your eyes and ears and busy yourself with distractions. Imagine what type of relationship that would turn into. Now, imagine that relationship being the one that you have with yourself. I know that for a large portion of my life that is exactly how I treated myself. I couldn't even tell you what my favorite color was, because the truth was, I didn't know. I never gave myself much thought. My thoughts were always geared to what I can do to make others happy.

The discovery of self, the love for self, starts with time with self. Again, for me, the first three Al-Anon steps encompass it all and it all comes down to being love. First you have to give yourself that love. Managing oneself is a full-time job all on its own and requires daily attention. The only way to do it is to stop and give yourself time. Every morning my act of self-love is creating that time and sacred space that I can sit with my morning reading and meditation and set the energy for my day. I finally understand and believe that I am enough all on my own.

"F.L.Y.- First Love Yourself. Others will come next."

- Unknown

QUESTIONS TO FACE YOURSELF

Who do you need to forgive?

Can you start with yourself?

How do you think it would feel to forgive yourself?

How can you start loving yourself more? What would that look like?

Be open to everything
and attached to
nothing.

- *Wayne Dyer*

Loving Again

There was something about him that felt like a breath of fresh air. His energy captivated everyone's attention when he walked in the room. He carried this carefree openness that was light, and it made everyone around him feel safe to be themselves. The moment I saw him, like everyone else, I was drawn in. "How could this man be so happy?" I thought to myself after meeting him because I knew he had just lost his wife. I wanted what he had. My soul yearned for it- I needed it. At that time, I was clawing at the skirts of life for direction, the exact recipe that would allow me to experience that inner happiness and connection to God that everyone raves about. Mike had it. I was tired of feeling how I always felt all my life- like I was on the inside looking out.

I asked Mike what his secret was, and he laughed but told me that he attends Alcoholics Anonymous since he was a recovering alcoholic and invited me to a meeting with him. Although I wasn't an alcoholic I agreed to go, and from there I learned about Al-Annon meetings which I then attended. Everyone at these meetings were so welcoming, so nonjudgmental, and they all exuberated peace. I knew that it was the exact place that I needed to be. The direction to happiness and healing that both meetings pointed to was to connect with a higher power (whatever that may be for each person), outside of ourselves to heal. Whether it's to heal an alcohol addiction or co-dependency addiction- the purpose was to heal. Not only heal, but heal that addiction feeling happier and more fulfilled; otherwise the healing will be short lived if living a life of addiction was more fulfilling, right?

Despite being deeply involved in church, I always felt half-full. During prayer nights, we'd throw oils and holy water all over the place, like we were the end all be all of everyone's problems; yet there I was absolutely miserable with my own life. After awhile it gets exhausting going through the motions, pretending to be someone that deep in your heart you know you are not, and having to act like everything is alright when it isn't. When you admit out loud that it isn't alright, you're instructed to have more faith, as if you don't have enough which leads to more shame and the feeling like you're not enough.

We both had lost our spouses. Even though Mike had lost his spouse in a different way than I had, we still connected at a soul level. He was my friend- a true friend. It really was a type of friendship with a male that I had never experienced before. I believe this is what allowed me to experience true intimacy with someone without there ever being sex involved, and that's rare.

That's what intimacy is though, a soul-level connection with another person without the initiation of any physical act. Intimacy means In-To-Me-You-See, and the feeling of not only being seen but understood is absolutely unexplainable. Imagine being at a crowded party, and you're sitting at a table in the corner watching everyone else dance, laugh, and be merry amongst themselves. Everyone else seems to be having a great time, but oddly enough no one takes notice of you nor stops to crack a smile or sit and talk. You sit there at this party we'll call life, day after day, month after month, year after year, wondering to yourself, "Is something wrong with me?" This is what most people feel like that have never experienced true intimacy-unseen and misunderstood.

Meeting Mike was my life altering moment because it was the first time, I got up from the table by myself and went out on the dance floor at this party of life and started dancing alone- regardless of who saw me or who I was with. Mike sparked that by just being him, by bringing light where he went, and pointing the direction for me to take to do the same.

With time, our friendship grew into something more, and it just felt right; yet there was this blockage in me that couldn't completely accept it, and now I see it's all because of my childhood trauma. I had almost become addicted to being unhappy and stuck. A part of me was holding on to what was already gone and the other part of me justifying it because I had to do things "right" and wait to move on with my life until the divorce was completely finalized. It didn't dawn on me until Mike had invited my children and I over to his house for Christmas, and instead of saying "absolutely," which is what I wanted, I called my ex-husband to ask permission. Yes, as odd as that sounds; I called my ex-husband to ask permission to take our kids to my boyfriend's house for Christmas, even though he had already moved on with his own life and had a girlfriend. That was the 'aha' moment that hit me like a ton of bricks, and I realized that it was time to move on and release this crazy belief system given to me by the church. This belief system that kept me addicted to the church and left me feeling as if like I needed approval and validation on every decision in my life.

My relationship with Mike helped me grow to the woman I am today. He showed me a rare love that I had never experienced up to that point in my life. A love that accepted me for who I was at that very moment, regardless of what issues or hang-ups I had. A love that made me feel safe to be myself, because I knew that either way, he'd love me. I didn't have to do anything. I didn't have to prove anything. All I had to do was just be me, and he'd remind me of that all the time until I believed him.

The foundation of our love was built on friendship and our self-development journey together. I really believe that was the glue. Finding someone you can grow with, not someone you stay stuck with, is the key to evolvement that leads to self-fulfillment.

"Those few people who don't project a mind-made image but function from the deeper core of their Being, those who do not attempt to appear more than they are but are simply themselves, stand out as 'remarkable'. They are the bringers of the new consciousness. Their mere presence- simple, natural, unassuming- has a transformational effect on whoever they come into contact with. When you don't play roles, it means there is not self (ego) in what you do. You are the most powerful, most effective, when you are completely yourself."

- Eckhart Tolle

My wedding day with Mike really did feel like a dream. We bought necklaces that had a cross on them for all the boys. He gave them to my sons, and I gave his sons theirs. The wedding and us giving them the necklaces were the initiation to all of us being a family. The necklaces were the symbol of us being united. A visual act and a tangible object made the unity of all of us being one even more real and erased any doubts that any of the boys may have had because now it wasn't just official for Mike and me, it was official for all of us.

The next day, our honeymoon, my youngest son reminded him that he had a basketball game and wanted to be sure he was going. Mike had volunteered as the coach and helped my son grow athletically in such a short amount of time. It was so important to Christian that Mike insisted that we spend our honeymoon at my son's basketball game. That was just the kind of guy he was. I not only respected him for it, but I admired him tremendously for all the rare characteristics he displayed daily, and not only to our family, but to the others as well. He was proof that the more you loved yourself, the more love, you had to give others.

"I don't trust people who don't love themselves and tell me, 'I love you. ' ... There is an African saying which is: Be careful when a naked person offers you a shirt, because if they had a shirt, they'd give it to themselves first."

- Maya Angelou

Every morning, he'd bring me coffee in bed, and we'd make our way into the living room, where we'd do our daily readings with each other and talk about what they meant to us. Although, we didn't have children together we were connected on a much deeper level that held such a high level of respect and honor for one another for who we were as individuals. Mike had a big personality, and like I said, he lit the room when he walked in, without even trying. That was just him, and I loved that about him. Understandably, for years, I lived in his shadow, and I was more than alright with it. I was safe in his shadow and following his lead. Naturally, when Mike got sick and we knew the end was approaching, I didn't know what I was going to do without him. He knew it too. Without me having to say anything, once again, he loaned me his confidence and reassured me that I would be alright and that I was enough, even without him. I looked in his eyes and it was as if he was telling me, "I got you this far, keep going-fly". In his eyes I gained his strength to get up and out of bed each day and keep going, to keep believing in myself, to keep growing, and searching inside of myself for what I too can give away to the world.

When he passed, I battled internally about how to move forward in life. Part of me wanted to condemn myself to a life of solitude out of pure loyalty to my late husband, and the other part of me knew he wanted me to take all that he taught me and heal, to surrender, to move forward with faith and an open heart. It took many mornings sitting in that same chair that he used to sit at having conversations with myself about what is next. I went to grief groups to gain insight to how other people handle similar situations, and it felt refreshing to know I wasn't alone and to be in a safe space to freely express myself with no judgement.

I've found that when we find ourselves at the crossroad of our own life, not knowing which direction to take, we try to find the one that has something to grasp that ensures safety. As human beings we long for security but sometimes things just aren't guaranteed. When we discover there are no guarantees, we're left only to retreat inside of ourselves and feel our way blindly through the dark. It is in this place that we find who we are, that we learn what our higher self wants for us. The unknown is scary to all of us. However, when you get the courage to face it rather than runaway in fear of it, something shifts. You'll find that curiosity will rise and that is when your heart will start to open to guide the way.

This is what I chose to do, because that is how Mike lived his life and I knew that he handed me the torch. After some time passed, I created an online dating site to get back out there and try to date instead of allowing myself to be a hermit for too long. I went on a date with a guy named, John. When he asked where I live, I knew the security rules and refused to tell him. I didn't know this guy. He decided to tell me first where he lived, and I couldn't believe what I was hearing. Out of all the men on that app, out of all the men in our city, he lived on my street- he was literally one of my neighbors across the street! Call it coincidence or chance but I believe it's nothing less than divinely orchestrated. John and I instantly clicked. Oddly enough, because John was our neighbor, he had met Mike years prior. I know that Mike must've had his spiritual hand in me and John meeting. The whole situation is not normal and pretty much unheard of, but hey, that seems to be the way my whole life has been up to this point.

This time around, though, it's as if my role in the relationship has reversed. I'm now in Mike's role while John is in the role I had in my relationship with Mike. I am now the widower with a lot of children, and he is me in regards to having a role that can't be replaced. It is so beautiful as we both learn how to navigate life in our new roles. Over time, the kids have even asked him if their children can give him a grandpa name.

Little did I know when I promised to continue his teachings and felt him pass the invisible torch of wisdom to me that it was very much real. My spiritual growth now continues the same path he did, continuing to pave the way to give to others while with each sunrise learning a deeper meaning of love by giving it to myself.

Every morning, I sit in that same chair that holds the energy of Mike reading to me every morning, that holds the energy of my tears, feeling lost, after he left us; that holds the energy of my heart open, feeling love once again. I sit in this chair and read over and over the first three Al Anon steps and ponder what it is that I need to surrender today? How can I be love? Each morning I feel the whispers of God, of Mike, of my angels, telling me to stay open. The more we release what is in our hand, is when the Almighty God can release what is in his to give to us. This requires us to do nothing but surrender.

QUESTIONS TO FACE YOURSELF

Who is your support group?

What do you need right now in terms of emotional support?

Can you let go and Trust the Universe/ Others who have gone before?

On our anniversary, after Mike's passing, I was in my garage looking for something in a box of random stuff and found a binder that had this letter to me to read after he died. Why he put it in a binder and stuck the binder in a box of random things, I'll never know? Even more crazy to think about is how I was led to go through a box of random things in my garage on my anniversary.

I put this in the book so that you would read it after I am gone. It is true. You will have a great life, not the same or without pain, but great, nonetheless.

My time with you was magical and the greatest period of my life. To watch you grow and flower into the true Rose of Sharon, was something to behold. I loved being part of it and to see the benefit of working the program in someone close to me. I never suggested it (well maybe more than go to one meeting a week) you were simply on your own quest to freedom and enlightenment. You will use it as you move into the next phase of your life. Always know that God has a plan for you greater than anything you can imagine. Also know that I loved you awesomely and wherever my spirit is, it is still looking over you and the kids. I loved you so much and hated to leave early, but that was God's plan for me. You are special and never forget that.

The message is God loves you, and I love you just the way you are. You're a precious child of God. You don't have to do anything, you don't have to prove anything, just be. I love you.
-Mike Hatch-

Suffering destroys the ego. Suffering has a noble purpose: the evolution of consciousness and the burning of the ego. The fire of suffering becomes the light of consciousness.

- *Eckhart Tolle*

Blood makes you related. Love makes you family.

- Unknown

Blending
Families

As most parents, I just wanted better for my kids than what I had growing up. I never wanted any of my children to feel as if they're always looking out the window waiting for me or wondering if I'll be there when they need me. I wanted to give them better and to me that meant giving my children a real family- the dad, the mom, the siblings, and the house with the picket fence; all of it. You know how life goes though. Most of the time, life has other plans for us in order for us to release our attachment to what we think we want. God always has the universe give us what we need first.

I needed to heal to show up as the mom that my children needed. For me to do that, I had to experience exactly what I didn't want and that was having a broken family with the father of my children. I had to experience watching my children wondering where their dad was just like I did as a child. I had to face my fears, my childhood fears, to heal them. Once I got to the point of being tired and unhappy it broke me free to look for answers. It broke me free from the fears that I had been trying so hard not to accept but had to come to terms with that I was not only facing it every day, but I was also living in it. Once I was free, I was open to attracting different, and that is when I met Mike. That's the thing about pain, it serves a purpose.

Now, you may be wondering what the heck does this have to do with blending a family. Well, it has everything to do with it because the more you heal as a parent, the better of a foundation you can create for a family to build on. Many blended families don't work as a family simply because they were trying to grow and build with each other on an unstable foundation.

Before I met Mike, I never could have imagined feeling the same love I had for my children for someone else's children. To my own surprise, I never even considered Mike's children my stepchildren, they were all my sons- all five of them. That was it. I didn't think twice about it. I probably couldn't have been at that place before though because the level of love that I gave myself at the time was limited; therefore, the love that I was capable of giving others was too. When I became open to more and was able to really receive love, it was then that I could also freely give it away. Love doesn't hold any titles or record or fear, our ego does. Leaving your ego at the door and being love everyday takes intention and work, with our own children or others. The first three Al-Anon steps really help me set that intention for myself everyday- reduce me to love.

"The best way to know God is to love many things."

- Vincent Van Gogh

When I was in the church prayer groups, all my church friends would come over my house to pray for a sick woman named Marti. It turned out that Marti was Mike's ex-wife, my stepsons' mother. I had never met Mike at that point, but I often wonder to myself what are the odds of that? When I was raising the boys, or even now in times of confusion or when I need to reflect, I'll go to my Marti's gravesite and speak with her as if we are old friends. During our talks in the silence of the cemetery, I've received many downloads of messages and gifts of peace to bring back home with me that only her spirit and I have a mutual understanding of. I am certain that I am able to receive these things only from remaining an active participant in my self-love journey so that I can love others at that level.

Creating a foundation for two different families to come together and build on all starts with the parents. You may disagree or even argue that we have to take into consideration our children's needs and opinions. All that is true, but the person that you decide to build a life with is ultimately your decision as the parent. Choosing a life partner is part of your right as an individual. Somehow as parents we lose our individuality at times and forget who we are and that we have rights too, and that always translates to the children feeling that way as well because they are a reflection of us. Mike taught me this by holding strong boundaries and put his self-care first, even with his children.

When he invited me and my two sons to his parent's house for Christmas, his oldest son apparently disagreed and remarked, "Oh, you're inviting them?" Mike stood firm in his decision and explained that who he decides to be in a relationship with is his decision. Unless that person is hurting them in some fashion then they don't get a say, because ultimately, they are going to grow up, move out, and find people who they will be in a relationship with someday. So, he is allowed to have the same right and as a family they need to respect his decision, and that was that. By Mike taking that stand, communicating that boundary to his sons, it set the tone for me to do the same, and for us to be the foundation, the glue, of the family. For Mike and I to be the sounding board for our children, together as a unit, meant that we had to continually be on the same page on our beliefs, perspectives, and filling our cup of self-love. This is why our morning ritual of reading and talking about daily devotional and life in general was so instrumental in us never growing apart or having different beliefs on how to deal with the family. A sounding board doesn't work if one part is away from the other.

There wasn't any talk amongst us about "your children" or "my children," it was "our children." The words we use dictate our beliefs and actions, so words that promote divisiveness must be eliminated for two families to become one. The only way that happens is through believing that you are one, and to do that, you must think that. When two people come together and try to lead the family with closed ears, that is a dictatorship and recipe for a disaster. When we want our children to respect our decisions and to really learn how to understand us as an individual, outside the lens of being their parent, that requires us to do the same for them. That means understanding our children are individuals too, and have their own opinions, needs, desires, dreams, and perspectives and they matter too. It requires us to open our ears and listen, to communicate. When big decisions needed to be made, Mike and I tried our very best to communicate it with the family and consider all our children's opinions. Each child mattered and contributed to the family in some function, and it made every one feel included, needed, and wanted, which is every human being's basic desires.

All of our children were dealing with their own struggles and losses. Mike's were still healing from their mother passing away. Mine had their own personal issues as well as learning to accept that we now have a different, bigger family. But each child felt safe and comfortable to express themselves in our home because the foundation, the sounding board, was solid and consistent. When the sounding board is wavy or unstable, so is the vibration throughout the household.

Before Mike passed away, we all stood around his bedside and made a promise to him that we'd stick together as a family; we would continue to love one another and be here for each other. He looked all of us in the eyes, one by one, and without saying one word, gave each of us the unseen knowing and strength to love each other even harder when he's gone because it's vital to the lasting of our family's progress. We all knew without having to say so. Lastly, he looked me in my eyes, and again, he had that way of communicating without having to say a word, he gave me the look that told me that he was handing the torch over to me. My last words to Mike were that I'd continue on with his teachings and ways with our family. That is how Mike lives on. That is the power of really healing and learning to love and care for yourself, you're able to touch the lives of everyone around you and lead them to do the same. That is legacy, and you can't put a price on that.

"People won't always remember what you have done, but they will always remember how you made them feel."

-Maya Angelou

After Mike left this world, I got up and left the bedroom. I hadn't eaten or gone to the restroom all day and I needed a break. When I returned, all five of our boys and one of their girlfriends were in the room standing around his bed. My son was playing the guitar, and they all were singing to Mike. I stood by the doorway in disbelief because it was so heart touching.

Januarys in Texas are normally cold and likely to even rain, but on the day of Mike's funeral the sky was clear blue. The sun was out that January afternoon like a summer day. During the funeral everything flowed so magically. I stepped to the side to look at the sea of faces of people that had attended and stood there in disbelief. There was well over a thousand people that came to pay their respect, and there wasn't a dry eye. Everyone had a story about Mike. Everyone had been positively impacted in one way or another by something he said or did. I was witnessing the power of love, the power what reducing me to love every day can really do. Love unites, it brings together, it breathes life even after death, it heals; and when two different families come together to be one, you need all of that.

I usually don't post things like this, but I think this time it is well deserved. Lakeway lost a great man this past week, and though I have been to many celebrations of life in the past, his was the best!

Mike was a recovered alcoholic. He missed his 30 year celebration of sobriety by three days, his birthday! I had no idea he had influenced so many alcoholics lives over the years! It had to be in the thousands! Mike knew everyone, and he was the type of guy you just wanted to be around. A man a few words, funny as hell, always the one on the dance floor loving life!!! The best part was he really had a great relationship with the Lord! That's who he leaned on daily to stay sober.

The celebration of life yesterday was amazing. My guess is 1500 attended ! Wow! At one point all of the people who were influenced through AA were asked to stand up, and I swear over half of the room stood ! We could all wish to have this kind of positive influence on others, and have a celebration of life like his!!

The best part to me was when his stepson, who is an incredible musician, sang Lynyrd Skynyrd "Simple Man". This was one of Mike's dying requests. There was not a dry eye in the house!

If I could influence 1/10 of the people Mike did, I'd die a happy man!

God Speed Hatch! I'll miss seeing who I called "the mayor of Lakeway" at the store, gym, and football games! I'm sure you are dancing in heaven!!

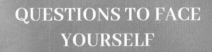

QUESTIONS TO FACE YOURSELF

What ways can you release expectations of others?

What ways can you show more love?

For you have come to
your position for such
a time as this.

- Esther 4:14

*Finding
Purpose
Through
Adversity*

L et's face it, bad things happen to everyone. There isn't one person walking this earth that hasn't been through some kind of trial and tribulation regardless of how much money or stature that they have. The difference is how we handle those trials. It may sound like a lofty expression or idea to surrender: to be love, to have faith, especially when you are in the middle of the greatest storm of your life trying to find cover. The truth really is that the most powerful thing you can do is to do nothing. You may be reading this and thinking, "Well that just sounds stupid." I would completely agree, because the thought of doing nothing when you're in the middle of a storm sounds completely reckless. The thing is, storms pass- they eventually end, and the rain fades away and the sun shines. Adversity works the same way.

Often when you are in the middle of something, it may overwhelm you and seem bigger than you. The truth is, something way greater is in charge and everything is greater than you and that is why we proceed to Al Anon's step two. You got yourself all the way up to this point, and there is no reason why you won't get yourself out. This time is no different than the last, but what can make the difference is how you handle it. Everything happening in life is a direct reflection of our reaction to it- everything! Letting go and praying then moving on to the next RIGHT thing is the answer, but how do you know what's right? Often, that takes time to realize, so learning how to pause is one of my greatest tools.

When Mike died, it didn't really seem like my life could have anymore emotional mountains to overcome, but hey, isn't that how life works? Right when you think you're on the other side, life throws something else at you and you look back and realize you've barely begun. That's how it was for me the day I was taken to the hospital after passing out for no apparent reason. After brain surgery, I learned I had a brain aneurysm. I was in the ICU for thirty days. My memory of being in the hospital is foggy. While in the hospital, I could feel myself slipping into dark places and felt the need to hold an Al-Anon meeting. The meetings, the support from my fellow like-minded friends, and the teachings are what has gotten me through the darkest hours of my life. There we were, in the ICU, with my head wrapped up from surgery, holding our meeting. To me, it was beautiful, and was exactly what I needed.

So, if you are reading this while experiencing some type of difficulty in life, I ask you, who is your support system? Who can you look to, to speak life over you, to fill your cup up when yours feels like it's running empty? Who can you rely on that will remind you to turn to God when things are difficult? If you don't have one, start looking for places that you can find them. That is the key to getting through difficult times and coming out on the other side even better. Often, we can get through it alone, but we come out of it all battered up and bitter. Everyone wants to get better though, not bitter, so the key is finding your support.

I had no idea how things at home were holding up without me. Any mother reading this understands that we are the ship that the family is on, and if the ship goes down, well, most of the time, everything else does too. John never left my side in the hospital, and although he wasn't legally allowed to make medical decisions for me, he did what he was able to do and continued to assure me that everything was alright. It was apparent to me that once again something good came out of something horrific in my life. John and the children were able to bond over the entire dilemma of me getting the aneurysm and being hospitalized. The children saw him step up and stay by my side, and that alone, spoke a million words. I realized that once again, I was experiencing the beauty of a new blended family and reminded how the cycle of what Mike started is still in continuation.

The survival rate of someone with a brain aneurysm was not in my favor, so the fact that I'm here today, writing this book is a miracle in itself. I've found a new sense of appreciation for life, for breathing, for being alive. Like Mike did after he got sober – now, like he was, I'm all emotional all the time– from pure gratitude to be alive. The question that has plagued me is, "Now what?" I've had to sit with that for a long time, and it repeatedly rang in my mind nonstop after I came home from the hospital, feeling completely useless to everyone. It was then that I realized that my identity has always been the roles I played in everyone's life around me, never the role that I play in my own life.

Now that everyone in my household stood up and took the reins of the situation while I was sick, I was incredibly proud and happy while also feeling confused as to where I was needed. It was an extremely eye-opening position to be in, because just when I felt like I had myself all figured out and like I could start planning what's next, there I was as lost and confused as the little girl looking out the window waiting for her parents to come home. I still didn't fully feel like I was enough, just being me and wondering why I didn't die if I wasn't meant to do for others. Even though Mike told me for years; even though I had faithfully attended Al-Anon meetings and sponsored many people and helped others in their healing journey; even though I was in my fifties, and I thought my inner child was healed already- the truth was that deep down that belief still lingered somewhere in me. It took almost dying, feeling useless in my own body and house to become aware of it. That's the thing about healing and evolving that I've learned, it's a never-ending spectrum of continually getting better than who we were yesterday. Sometimes we close a chapter in our healing journey thinking we're done and ready to move onto the next chapter, but life will have a way of showing you if you don't take time to make sure yourself. It was then that I realized that it was time to really feel like I was enough, to feel worthy for just being me, to show up for myself and myself alone.

I found the answer as to why I am still here and it's to continually unlock myself and heal and give back to others so they can feel inspired to do the same. I'm stepping out of the shadows of Mike, my past, my family, all my limiting beliefs and seeing who I am with no filter. Losing Mike and surviving a brain aneurysm a few years later taught me that finding the lessons in hardship is how we also get through adversity better. We grow through something we learn from, or we go back and repeat it if we don't, because cycles are classes in life meant to graduate us to the next level once we learn the lesson.

I placed Oprah's quote earlier in the book about life whispering to us, and that is something that I whole heartedly believe. Just like she so eloquently stated, life has stages of how it speaks to us: first in whispers, then a flick in the head, and if we still don't get it, then a brick. After realizing the lesson and recovering from the brain aneurysm I started looking for the whispers, the flicks from life that I missed. Sure enough, they were there. It's so mind blowing how an entire experience can look different when you view through the filter of the lesson. When Mike was dying, I took over his businesses even though I had no idea what I was doing, I was determined to learn as Mike instructed me along the way. Yes, I was nervous. Yes, I was overwhelmed. Yes, I was every emotion you can imagine, and what I realize is when you're in the thick of something it's hard to see the lesson because you're just trying to get through it. We've all been there, but I realize more than ever how important it is to stay neutral, stay in the middle and not be in the extremes, especially on the daily. One particular business of Mike's was a medical building and Mike didn't want everyone to know he was dying because of the chaos it would cause. After he passed, I had to tell them that they had to get a new management company because I couldn't do it anymore. The morning I was to go there to clean up all the files in his office and meet with the Executives and CEO's I had an emotional breakdown in the car and had to pull the car over on the side of the freeway. That was the moment life whispered to me, or maybe it was a flick, but it was something for me to look further into. I felt like there I was, this little girl who received free lunches at school, going to meet with CEO's and Executives, and I didn't know anything about running a big business like that one. I thought to myself, "What am I doing?!" As the tears rolled down my face I started hyperventilating and called my good friend as I sat in the car crying. Once again, I didn't feel like I was enough. I related myself to the little girl I was in my childhood, and it was still the determining factor of my worthiness. My level of worthiness caused this inner battle because I wanted to make Mike proud and things right for him.

Nobody in the meeting that day would have been able to tell that I just had an emotional breakdown an hour earlier. Nobody would've been able to see the conflicting storm taking place in my inner world. Isn't that how it is in life for everyone though? We never know what anyone else is going through, what kind of storm is taking place in their inner world. Therefore, be intentional about judging no one and having compassion for everyone. Regardless, of how far I've come in my life, I still had work to do on my worthiness, feeling like I am enough. My inner child was still crying out to me through the noise of my grief and losses in life, and I am now being extremely intentional about taking time tending to her. Reflecting on Al-Anon's fourth step has helped me gain a lot of clarity on myself and the lesson through this. That is, what can you learn about yourself through the experience? It is reflecting on the lessons, not just from the moments that life threw us bricks, but also through the whispers and flicks. I encourage you, to ask yourself, what whispers and flickers from life did you perhaps miss, and what was the lesson that life wanted to teach you?

Since I have experienced many whispers, flickers, and bricks by life, adversity if you call it, I am able to relate to more people. Adversity molds us and gives us wisdom because diamonds are only made under pressure. The more wisdom you gain, ultimately means, the more people you can help, the more impact you can have. What can you do to help the most people with what you've learned? Giving it away is what ultimately fills your cup back up while filling others that thirst for what you know. Seek the lessons, gain the wisdom, give it away, repeat.

QUESTIONS TO FACE YOURSELF

What did you learn through each experience of adversity that you experienced?

What can you create with what you learned?

Who can you help with the wisdom you gained?

I understood myself
only after I destroyed
myself. And only in
the process of fixing
myself, did I know
who I really was.

- Unknown

Addiction

It's the thief in the night that creeps in through a forgotten unlocked window left barely cracked enough to be noticed only by someone looking for a way in. When it comes in, it crawls to the bed, slowly and quietly, never to be noticed or heard, and before you can open your eyes, its cold hand is around your throat squeezing with all it's might, restricting your air flow. Your face turns blue, your mind is discombobulated, your eyes roll back, and just when you think it's over, it loosens its death grip, but only long enough for you to gasp for just enough air to keep the process going. Addiction is the thief in the night that secretly lives in almost every home, every family, in one way or another.

Many families are so hush about it, never wanting to talk or even admit about what's really going on behind closed doors out of shame and embarrassment that they left a way in. Consequently, the birth of the mask makes its entry to that family, and they all play their role to the outside world, and in their attempt to convince the world that everything is alright, they too fall into the abyss of their delusions and lies. You may ask when does it end or how does it end? The real question though is why did it start?

In our society, drugs, alcohol, tobacco, and prescription drugs are the stamp for addiction. This is what we're shown, we're taught, and what registers when one speaks of addiction. We say we understand, but do we really? The truth is even scarier than people care to see but as I've repeatedly stated throughout this book, it's only in recognizing the truth do we set ourselves free to continue in our truth how we want. The truth is that addiction comes in not only the form of substance abuse but in many other areas as well. Most of us have codependency, which is an addiction. That is, the reliance of something or someone outside of yourself for validation. A lot of us in one way or another are addicted to suffering. Most of the time, we are completely unconscious to it. Consequently, in some form or another we sabotage an area of our life.

It is only through recognizing you have an addiction, then understanding the root issue of how it arrived in your life, do you start the journey of freeing yourself from it. My flavor of addiction happens to be codependency. Mike's was alcohol and was passed down to him biologically despite having great, supportive parents. Mine was my survival mechanism as a child and coping mechanism from all the unhealed childhood wounds. The constant, never-ending search for outside validation left me exhausted, depleted, and burned out very much like a substance addict. Although we both had two different types of addictions that were brought on in different ways, addressing them at the root issue is key because otherwise you're just placing a band aid over the wound. Often, it's only after being stuck in a mess that we've created for so long that we wake up long enough to realize that we need to confront the issue to change and create a new cycle.

Usually there is one person in a family that is given the will and strength of self-actualization to forge the path to end the cycle of addiction in their bloodline. In this process, an energy is triggered within the family, and much like a domino effect, one by one, limiting beliefs, all the ways of suffering, family secrets, and darkness is knocked down thus simultaneously revealing itself. It's not an easy path or process and not just anyone can start it in a family. It's often lonely and difficult but the wisdom you gain is what ultimately has impact. Not everyone is saved even when they do the work, but the energy you create by trying isn't in vain. It plants seeds in yourself for future use and is also passed down to your children and family. Those of us that forge this path in our families want to believe that the work stops with us. That it's done. The scary truth is that often there is still much more work needed to rid our bloodline of this dark force, and so it continues with our children.

That is what happened to me. I never thought or even wanted to imagine I'd see the day that one of my sons was an addict, but I did, and I know it was because I had the tools to help him that he received the strength to heal. My son, Vincent, the musician in our family, a unique ear for music, a true creative as well as an empath leaving him extremely sensitive to the energy around him, suffered from heroin addiction. I had no idea what was going on although there were signs that I missed because I perceived them as typical teenager behavior. Sadly, it turned out to be so much more than that, but it wasn't until after Mike's death that I discovered the truth when he came to live with me. He was so high that it was impossible to mistake or deny. He had lost his apartment, had no money, and even went as far as pawning his guitar to get his fix before a show that he wanted to perform at. I helplessly stood by and watched my son, my baby, go through the process of gasping for air and being choked again. I did what I knew how to do- I turned to the Al Anon steps and sat with myself to create the boundaries that I knew I needed for my own peace. I knew that this meant that I'd have to follow through with them even if that meant putting my son out on the streets. After losing my husband, I couldn't possibly imagine losing my son too, but I remembered that to whom much is given, much is expected, and I wasn't going to lose my son without a fight.

Making your words count to an addict that is high really comes down to your actions; otherwise, all they are, are words. Even if the person was this caring, loving individual when sober or before their addiction, all that changes when the death grip of addiction is in the equation. It hurts. It's devastating. It strips you of all your power, especially as a mother, and leaves you feeling helpless, wondering where you went wrong. If you've experienced this, please know, you are not alone and because it's this way now, doesn't mean it'll stay this way forever. Yet, focusing on what you do have control of is key, and that always starts with creating your boundaries. This is how Al-Anon really helped mold my brain to retract to that mindset under pressure. With my son, my boundary was that he could not live with me while high. Even though it was right after Mike had passed and I was still dealing with my grief, I am proud of myself for being confident and firm in the boundaries I immediately created. I knew that he needed to detox somewhere though, and I knew that would require assistance from someone. I watched him desperately look for his guitar in the garage to pawn so he could get money to get high which was necessary for him to be able to perform at a show that evening. My heart sank that it had gotten this bad, and I looked my son in the eyes, and told him in the most stern, loving voice that I knew he had a problem and that he could not live in the house unless he was sober.

I could see that he wanted to get sober, that he feared being homeless, but he just didn't know how. The same guy that Mike had helped years before to get sober had agreed to take my son in to detox; another full circle moment out of many that brings so much gratitude to my heart.

Often, even if an addict wants to get sober, the death grip of drugs is stronger and completely takes over. If given the freedom and opportunity to use, more than likely, they will, even if they don't want to, even if they promised, even if all is on the line. Remember, it's not personal, it's the addiction. Even when faced with being thrown out of the only place he had to live and being homeless, he still tried to use. He thought he could be slick and pretend his way through a fake sobriety, but it was only a few days before our family friend caught on. He was given one warning, and he knew then things were serious. For the next two weeks he was isolated to detox, and he got through it. He not only got through it, but he did the work after to stay sober. My son is now five years clean and a successful musician who was signed to a label during a pandemic that openly shares this experience to help others.

I know this isn't every addict's story. I know that for many it feels impossible to have any hope. Like any traumatic experience, I challenge you to look at this experience in your life a little differently for you to gain a new perspective. This experience is one of the many classes that you were enrolled in to take in this school of life. What are the lessons that you learned in this class and how have you applied them to your life? The healing begins here, and it is here that the energy that you create through healing is passed down to our children and grandchildren. The process of healing from any type of trauma forces us at some point to face ourselves. It is in this process alone that we can clearly see who we are in our own reflection, and it is then that we can take back control of our lives. It is then that you can change what needs to be changed. Tony Robbins says, "Whatever you focus on grows," the same holds true to every situation. Focus on the problem, it'll expand and grow. Or focus on what you have control of- which is you- and watch the growth.

Unfortunately, there is no handbook or quick fix remedy for dealing with addiction or supporting a loved one who is struggling with addiction, but surrounding yourself with people that understand, that have been through it all before, is why Al Anon has been so helpful for me. What we do have instead of a "How to Handbook" are Universal Laws that can be applied to any situation. I've recognized that through all the different struggles and adversities I've been through, there was always one direction they were pointing me to-myself. Everything has forced me to turn inward, dig deep, and find the little girl that is still hurt inside of me, and give her more and more love as I continue on this journey. In facing myself, I have discovered in every class that the lesson is to learn how to love me.

Sometimes holding on, does more damage than letting go.

- Unknown

QUESTIONS TO FACE YOURSELF

What form of suffering do you recognize cycles
of in you and your family?

How is this form of suffering impacting your life?

Why do you think you've held onto it?

What would it look like to release it?

Our life is like a house. In order for us to make space for the new furniture we desire to bring into our house, we must take out the old furniture.

- Jen the Rainmaker

Letting Go

All of us have experienced something in life that we have had difficulty getting past and letting go. Some of us more than others. As simple as it sounds, it's not, and, in fact, letting go is an art. Yes, an art. All of us have our own way of doing it that feels right. Some of us are still in the learning phase of what our style is exactly. I believe that those of us that have experienced abandonment and neglect from our parents, like I have, tend to hold on a little tighter to things that we love or things that are comfortable, and often the two can become mixed up. What is comfortable doesn't always mean it's healthy for us because trauma can feel comfortable when you've been raised in it. Often, it is the comfortable furniture in our house that needs to be tossed out in order for us to bring the new plush furniture in.

The big question is how do you let go? I wish it was as easy as waking up and saying to yourself that you're going to let go, but I believe that it can be if we say it will be. Making a decision that it is time is a powerful force. Sometimes to get to that point, you have to experience holding on to something that is too burdensome, too painful, too heavy to carry any longer. It is then that we decide that it is time to let go, and it is then that we seek for our way of doing it.

"There is nothing as powerful as a changed mind."

- Reverend T.D. Jakes

I've replayed in my mind on repeat for years looking out the window as a little girl, waiting for my dad to come home. Experiencing again and again the confusion, the sadness, the emptiness that I felt wanting to be held and loved by my dad and most of all, my mom. I've replayed in my mind, experiencing the same thing with my first husband, waiting for him to come home and be with me and the kids, experiencing the same emptiness and sadness, grasping for straws of what I could do next to make him stay. I've replayed in my mind sitting with my mom as she took her last breath, wishing there was more time to make up for all that was lost between us. I've replayed in my mind, Mike leaving me, the look in his eyes as he whispered his last words to me, holding his hand as he left this world. These memories are now a part of me, embedded in my soul, on standby waiting to be played and recognized at the first chance of availability in my mind. It wasn't until letting Mike go that I realized how to step out of being vulnerable to the memories that are on standby ready to play on repeat, triggering the same emotions within me to surface. It was a process to get here; to a place of accepting of what it is instead of focusing on what it should be.

When I found myself experiencing the same exact cycle with my ex-husband that I did with my parents, I knew that it clearly stemmed from childhood trauma; yet I didn't know how to stop it. I had no clue of how to go about changing what I was feeling or felt compelled to do, so instead, I clung onto hope that it will all be different one day and continued to persist. I covered my truth in denial that was justified by the church teaching me that a wife does not leave her husband but rather fights for the marriage. I distracted myself from facing the truth by trying to be the picture perfect, church going wife. When all else failed and there wasn't anything else I could possibly do but face the truth, I then did. The hope that I created out of nothing but delusions in my mind, had become too much of a burden to continue to carry and it was then that I decided to set them down, to let go, and took a chance to open myself up to love again; most importantly, first learning how to love myself. Self-love has been the foundation for healing all the strained relationships in my life, especially the one with my mother.

The emotions towards my mom have always been tumultuous, but as I continued my journey with Al Anon, priming my mind to learn acceptance, less resentment and more compassion started to develop towards her. We'd talk on the phone once or month or so. The connection was never deep, but I didn't know how to go about creating it because she always felt so distant and emotionally unavailable. When I was told she was too old and frail to care for herself, I agreed to take her in.

Mike took the lead and drove to Massachusetts to pick her up and bring her back to our home for me to care for her. Suddenly, the roles had reversed. The daughter had become the mother, and through mothering her, I gained invaluable insight to understanding my mother on a much deeper level. The understanding washed away any lingering hurt, sadness, resentment, or anger towards her. It allowed me to not only show her unconditional love but to be grateful that I learned tools to start healing. The energy of trauma is a real thing, and it lingers and haunts a family until someone stands up and turns the light on to see it for what it is and does the work to end it.

Eventually, I had to put my mother into a fulltime care center because she was diagnosed with cancer and required more help than I could give, and she did what she always would do, maintain her distance from everyone until she was completely isolated. The blessing in disguise was that she could no longer run away because of her health, leaving her with no choice but to accept the love that my family wanted to give. My son, Vincent, would visit her every day and help take care of her. It was a beautiful thing and I believe the beginning of healing for her, me, and him. I was able to spend time with her and continue to show her love. I understood what she was feeling and wanted her to know that all was forgiven, all is alright, that she is worthy of love, she no longer needs to carry the burden of guilt, and as she took her last breath holding my hand, everything came to full circle. I became the mother that came to the little girl in my mother waiting for love. It was then that my art of letting go changed to doing through understanding.

Mike's death triggered so many emotions to surface for me, but mostly it was the struggle I faced with accepting that he was gone, letting him go. I've spent years doing the steps with Al-Anon to understand acceptance, but when faced by it through the death of my husband that I loved dearly, I was left confused as to how to really do it. Through my morning routine and deep reflection, I began to see that resisting the acceptance of his death is too much of a burden, and I clearly understood the mission that he passed to me on his death bed, and there was no other choice but to release all resistance towards what I wanted it to be. I've allowed myself to grieve, to cry, to be angry, to be lost, and feel lonely. I've stopped fighting the emotions that want to hide within me, because how can any of us let go when we're hiding from what wants to be released?

> "If you're going through hell, keep going. Why would you stop in hell?"
>
> - **Steve Harvey**

Yet, once again, I've been left to face myself through the reflection of grief and letting Mike go, and I see myself in such a different light. I think people that have experienced many losses are forced to do this again and again, consciously, or not, and at some point, find themselves finally seeing who they really are. I saw myself want to emerge from the shadows that I've lived in my entire life, and create my own mission, my own path, forged from all that I've gathered in my many journeys in this lifetime. I now understand that letting go is an art that evolves through time by creating something to help others with the pain from the experiences you had in your journey. The life-altering question that I've asked myself that shifted my perspective is "What can I create with what I have right now to make my life better, to make other people's lives better, to make the world better?" I challenge you to ask yourself the same question and get curious to what path it leads you down and I promise you'll find yourself experiencing life through the eyes of a child seeing something for the first time. You'll find yourself enjoying the journey.

QUESTIONS TO FACE YOURSELF

What does it look like when you let go?

What do you think you need to let go of in present day?

How would it help you and others lives?

Accept what is.
Let go of what was.
Have faith in what
will be.

- Shareen Rivera

About the
Author

Sharon Hatch is a serial entrepreneur that has set the intention to contribute to raising the vibration of the collective by following without questioning the calling and clues sent to her by spirit. Sharing her story through writing a book after having extreme memory loss from having a brain aneurysm would seem nothing but short from crazy to everyone else, but she listened to the calling. Through the process of digging within to remember, she found her voice that she is paving the path to use to help others navigate their journey, overcome adversity, and become empowered by the person they are. It all starts with facing yourself.

You can reach Sharon via email or her website:
www.sharonhatch.com
sharon.s.hatch@gmail.com

Made in the USA
Columbia, SC
25 October 2022

69947307R00065